FOOTSTEPS IN TIME

THE Inuit

Ruth Thomson

Contents

Children's Press
A Division of Grolier Publishing
New York • London • Hong Kong • Sydney
Danbury, Connecticut

12/97

Who are the Inuit?

Inuit people live in northern Canada, Alaska, Greenland, and on the eastern tip of Siberia. In the past, the Inuit survived by fishing and by hunting whales, seal, and caribou. The animals provided them with food and materials for clothing, shelter, light, tools, transportation, weapons, and heat.

Today, most Inuit families live in modern houses. They can buy everything they need from stores. Many live in towns and communities where there are jobs and modern facilities. Wherever they live, the Inuit are trying to make their lives better by reclaiming their land and taking greater control of it.

An ivory carving

For centuries, the Inuit have been skilled craftsmen. They make beautiful carvings of wood, bone, stone, and ivory.

You will need:

Black crayon   Scissors   Cardboard

Follow the steps . . .

1. Cut a piece of cardboard in the shape of a walrus tusk.

2. Draw scenes of Inuit life on it. You could show people hunting or fishing. You might like to show their summer camp with tents.

Hunting

In the past, the Inuit moved from place to place, hunting animals on foot.

In spring and summer they hunted seal and walrus from boats called kayaks. They speared them with harpoons and killed only what they needed. All year round they fished in lakes and streams.

Now the Inuit can buy food and clothes in stores. They work during the week. Many Inuit still hunt and fish for their own food on weekends. They are keeping alive the skills of the past and teaching them to their children.

Many Inuit travel by snowmobile or motor boat and hunt with rifles. Others prefer to use dog sleds and traditional weapons.

A sled

You will need:

Balsa wood	Thick cardboard	Fabric scraps
Scissors	Paint and brush	String
Styrofoam chips	Sandpaper	Glue

Follow the steps . . .

1. For the runners, ask an adult to cut two strips of balsa wood, 10 inches by 1 inch. Sandpaper one edge to make it curved, like this.

2. Cut and paint several strips of cardboard, 2 inches long by 1 inch wide. Glue them along the runners.

3. Roll up some fabric scraps and glue them to the sled. Add some snow blocks made of Styrofoam.

4. Glue string to both runners.

An Arctic frieze

The Inuit respected the animals they hunted and decorated their weapons with pictures of them.

You will need:

White paper   Paints and brush   Scissors
Pencil   Glue

Follow the steps . . .

1. Sketch the background for your frieze in pencil and paint it.

2. Paint and cut out some Arctic animals and birds.

3. Glue them onto the background.

4. You could add an Inuit as well.

Clothing

The Inuit wear warm clothes for ten months of the year. Inuit women still make many clothes from animal skins. It takes time to prepare the skins. They scrape and clean the skins. Later, they chew them to make them soft. Then they sew the clothes with tight stitches to make them waterproof.

Trousers and hooded coats, called parkas, are made from caribou and polar bear skin. Mittens and boots are made of sealskin or polar bear fur. Under these outer clothes, the Inuit wear another layer of soft fur clothes.

Many Inuit wear modern clothes at home, but they still wear furs when they go hunting.

Mittens

You will need:

Needle and thread   Pencil   Cardboard   Scissors
Pieces of felt   Ribbon   Cotton wool   Pins

Follow the steps . . .

1. Put your hand on the cardboard and draw an outline around it. Draw another line 8 inches outside your hand shape. Cut along this outer line.

2. Fold some felt in half. Pin the cardboard hand to it. Cut through both layers of felt, around the hand shape. Turn the hand over and repeat step 2.

3. Sew each pair of felt pieces together. Turn them inside out. Sew cotton wool around the wrists.

Inuit collage

You will need:

White cardboard   Brown paper   Black felt
Cotton wool   Fabric scraps   Gluc
Felt-tip pens   String

Follow the steps . . .

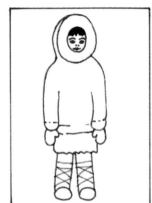

1. Draw an Inuit figure on white
   cardboard. Give him or her
   a face and black felt hair.

2. Cut out a brown paper parka,
   fabric trousers, boots, and mittens.
   Glue them on to your figure.

3. Decorate with cotton
   wool and string.

Homes

The Inuit live in communities that include stores, schools, churches, and sports centers.

Their wooden houses are brought in from cities, already partly made. The houses have central heating and triple glazing to keep them warm. They are built on stilts, so that heat from inside does not melt the frozen ground beneath.

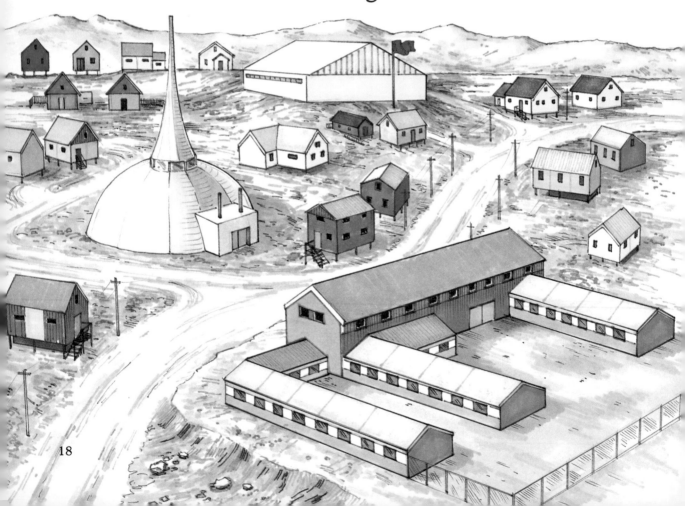

In the past, the Inuit lived in sod houses with roofs thatched over beams of whalebone.

During winter hunting trips, they built snowhouses. These were heated with seal-oil lamps and had a sleeping platform of snow. A tunnel entrance kept the cold wind out. In summer, they lived in tents made of skins.

Snowhouse

You will need:

Balloon	Bowl of water	Newspaper
Glue	Scissors	Cardboard
White paint	Paintbrush	Salt

Follow the steps . . .

1. Blow up a balloon. Cover half of it with newspaper strips, dipped in a mixture of glue and water. Let it dry.

2. Pop the balloon and remove it. Trim the rim of the dome. Cut a doorway. Snip the edges.

3. Cut a cardboard shape like this, with the flat edge about 6 inches long. Bend and glue it to the doorway.

4. Paint your snowhouse white. While it is wet, sprinkle on salt to make it glisten.

Games

On dark winter days, when bad weather kept them inside, the Inuit used to play homemade games.

You will need:

Self-hardening or oven-baked clay   Modeling tools

Follow the steps . . .

1. Sculpt some small Arctic animals and people from clay. Make sure each one has a wide, flat base. Let them dry.

2. Take turns throwing your models into the air.

3. You get one point each time one of your pieces lands upright. The winner is the first player to get 30 points.

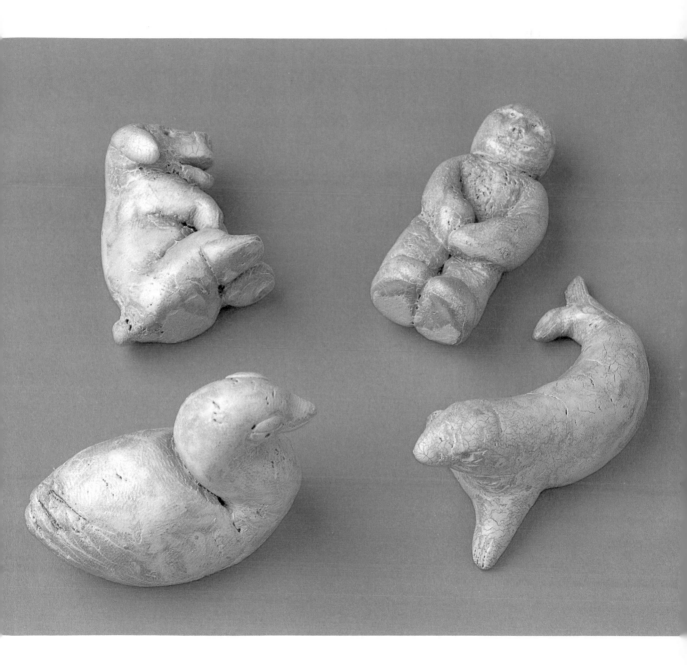

INDEX

Entries in *italics* are activity pages.

© 1996 Watts Books, London, Sydney
All rights reserved. Printed in Malaysia.
Published simultaneously in Canada
1 2 3 4 5 R 99 98 97 96 95 94

SeriesEditor: Annabel Martin
Consultant: Keith Lye
Design: Ruth Levy
Artwork: Cilla Eurich and Ruth Levy
Photographs: Peter Millard

First American Edition © 1996 by Children's Press
A Division of Grolier Publishing
Sherman Turnpike
Danbury CT 06816

Thomson, Ruth.
    The Inuit / Ruth Thomson
        p. cm. -- (Footsteps in time)
    Summary: Describes the traditional way of life of the Inuit.
Includes activities in which common items represent what the Inuit
used, such as making a snowhouse out of newspapers.
        ISBN 0-516-08072-5
    1. Inuit--Social life and customs--Juvenile literature. 2. Inuit-
-Material culture--Juvenile literature. 3. Creative activities and
seat work--Juvenile literature. [1. Inuit--Social life and customs.
2. Eskimos--Social life and customs. 3. Handicraft.]
    I. Title. II.Series
    E99.E7T5 1996
    970.004'971--dc20   95-25253
                                          CIP AC